3 1110 00206 3881

D1306503

Owen's O Book

WRITTEN BY **J. L. MAZZEO**
ILLUSTRATED BY **HELEN ROSS REVUTSKY**

dingles & company New Jersey

First Printing

Published By dingles&company
P.O. Box 508
Sea Girt, New Jersey 08750

LIBRARY OF CONGRESS CATALOG CARD NUMBER
2005907210

ISBN
ISBN-13: 978 1-59646-500-8
ISBN-10: 1-59646-500-X

Printed in the United States of America

My Letter Library series is based on the original concept of Judy Mazzeo Zocchi.

ART DIRECTION
Barbie Lambert & Rizco Design
DESIGN
Rizco Design
EDITED BY
Andrea Curley
PROJECT MANAGER
Lisa Aldorasi
EDUCATIONAL CONSULTANT
Maura Ruane McKenna
PRE-PRESS BY
Pixel Graphics

EXPLORE THE LETTERS OF THE ALPHABET WITH MY LETTER LIBRARY*

Aimee's **A** Book
Bebe's **B** Book
Cassie's **C** Book
Delia's **D** Book
Emma's **E** Book
Faye's **F** Book
George's **G** Book
Henry's **H** Book
Izzy's **I** Book
Jade's **J** Book
Kelsey's **K** Book
Logan's **L** Book
Mia's **M** Book
Nate's **N** Book
Owen's **O** Book
Peter's **P** Book
Quinn's **Q** Book
Rosie's **R** Book
Sofie's **S** Book
Tad's **T** Book
Uri's **U** Book
Vera's **V** Book
Will's **W** Book
Xavia's **X** Book
Yola's **Y** Book
Zach's **Z** Book

* All titles also available in bilingual English/Spanish versions.

WEBSITE
www.dingles.com
E-MAIL
info@dingles.com

My **Letter** Library

O o

My Letter Library leads young children through the alphabet one letter at a time. By focusing on an individual letter in each book, the series allows youngsters to identify and absorb the concept of each letter thoroughly before being introduced to the next. In addition, it invites them to look around and discover where objects beginning with the specific letter appear in their own world.

Aa Bb Cc Dd Ee Ff Gg

Hh Ii Jj Kk Ll Mm Nn

Oo Pp Qq Rr Ss Tt Uu

Vv Ww Xx Yy Zz

O is for Owen.

Owen is an observant owl.

On Owen's perch
you will find an oil lamp,

oats in a jar,

and odorous onions
to fry for dinner.

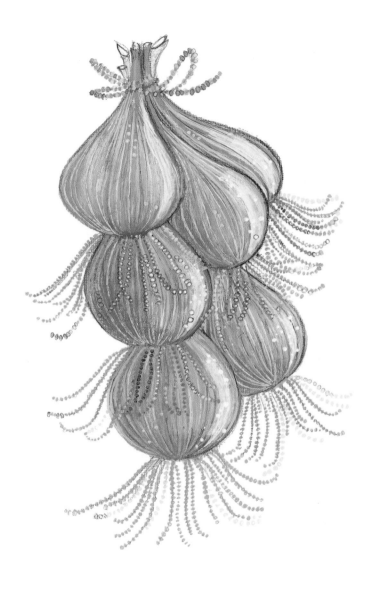

From Owen's perch
you can see an old oak tree,

an ornery osprey
named Oliver,

Oo

and an **o**riole

who loves to fly.

Near Owen's perch
you will find an orchid
that smells like perfume,

some oranges from Florida,

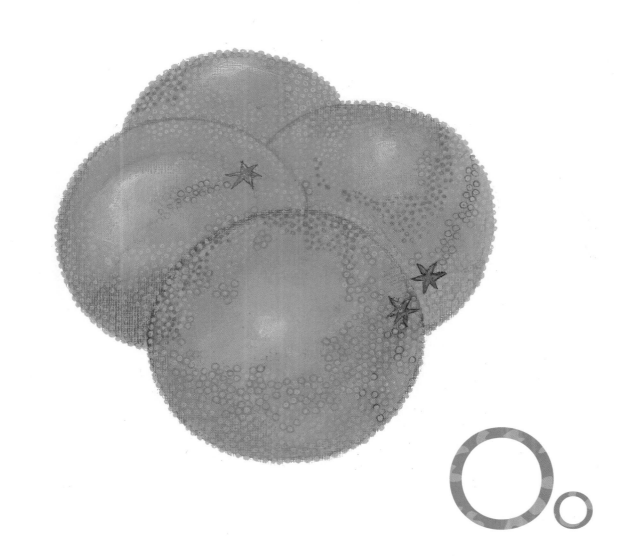

and an **o**possum

who is getting ready

for bed.

Oo

Things that begin with
the letter O are all around.

OIL LAMP

OATS IN A JAR

ONIONS

OAK TREE

OSPREY

ORIOLE

ORCHID

ORANGES

OPOSSUM

Where near Owen's perch
can they be found?

Have an "O" Day!

Read "O" stories all day long.

Read books about owls, oak trees, onions, orchids, and other **O** words. Then have the child pick out all of the words and pictures starting with the letter **O**.

Make an "O" Craft: An Owl Puppet

Cut a hole in one side of a toilet tissue tube near the bottom with a pair of scissors.

Have the child use crayons or washable markers to color the tube brown to resemble a tree trunk.

Draw an owl's face on the child's index finger using a washable marker. Show the child how to poke his or her finger through the hole so it looks as if an owl is peeking out of a hollow tree.

Enjoy the **"O"** Owl Puppet.

Make an "O" Snack: Octopus Sandwiches

- Place several slices of bread on a flat surface.
- Press the mouth of a medium-sized cup on top of a slice of bread and twist the cup back and forth. Remove the circle you made with the cup from the bread slice. Repeat for each slice.
- Have the child spread his or her favorite topping (peanut butter, jelly, cream cheese, etc.) on the circles. Then have him or her add raisins, nuts, olives, or grapes for eyes, a nose, and a mouth.
- Slice celery or carrot sticks into thin strips and have the child place eight sticks around each circle to make legs for the Octopus Sandwiches!

For additional **"O"** Day ideas and a reading list, go to www.dingles.com.

About **Letters**

Use the My Letter Library series to teach a child to identify letters and recognize the sounds they make by hearing them used and repeated in each story.

Ask:
- What letter is this book about?
- Can you name all of the **O** pictures on each page?
- Which **O** picture is your favorite? Why?
- Can you find all of the words in this book that begin with the letter **O**?

ENVIRONMENT

Discuss objects that begin with the letter **O** in the child's immediate surroundings and environment.

Use these questions to further the conversation:
- Have you ever seen a real owl?
- Do you have oak trees in your neighborhood?
- Have you ever eaten an onion? If so, how did it taste?

OBSERVATIONS

The My Letter Library series can be used to enhance the child's imagination. Encourage the child to look around and tell you what he or she sees.

Ask:
- Pretend you are an owl. Where would you fly at night?
- What would you do if you stayed up late?
- What is your favorite **O** object at home? Why?
- Where do owls live?

TRY SOMETHING NEW...

The next time you are at a park or lake, ask a parent if you can bring some birdseed. Be sure not to sprinkle it too close to the swings or picnic area.

J. L. MAZZEO grew up in Middletown, New Jersey, as part of a close-knit Italian American family. She currently resides in Monmouth County, New Jersey, and still remains close to family members in heart and home.

HELEN ROSS REVUTSKY was born in St. Petersburg, Russia, where she received a degree in stage artistry/ design. She worked as the directing artist in Kiev's famous Governmental Puppet Theatre. Her first book, *I Can Read the Alphabet,* was published in Moscow in 1998. Helen now lives in London, where she has illustrated several children's books.